D1565973

Mary Decker Slaney

By
Matthew Newman

Edited By
Dr. Howard Schroeder
Professor in Reading and Language Arts
Dept. of Elementary Education
Mankato State University

Produced & Designed By

Baker Street Productions, Ltd.

CRESTWOOD HOUSE
Mankato, Minnesota
U.S.A.

LIBRARY OF CONGRESS CATALOGING-IN-PUBLICATION DATA

Newman, Matthew.
  Mary Decker Slaney.

  (SCU-2)
  SUMMARY: Follows the champion runner from her first race at the age of eleven
to her recognition as one of the top runners in the world.
  1. Decker, Mary, 1958-   — Juvenile literature. 2. Runners (Sports) — United
States — Biography — Juvenile literature. (1. Decker, Mary, 1958-   . 2. Runners
(Sports). I. Schroeder, Howard. II. Title. III. Series: Sports Close-ups.
  GV1061.15.D42N48   1986   796.4'26   (B)   (92)   86-16525
  ISBN 0-89686-319-0

International Standard Book Number: 0-89686-319-0	Library of Congress Catalog Card Number: 86-16525

PHOTO CREDITS

Cover: Warren Morgan/Focus On Sports
Focus On Sports: 4
Carl Iwasoki/Sports Illustrated: 7, 14
Tony Mangia/Sports Chrome: 8
UPI/Bettmann Newsphotos: 11, 22, 43
Mitchell B. Reibel/Sports Chrome: 17
Heinz Kluetmeier/Sports Illustrated: 18
AP/Wide World Photos: 25, 31, 46

John Jacono/Sports Illustrated: 27
Steve Pruell/Sports Illustrated: 29, 30
Brian Lanker/Sports Illustrated: 32, 33, 34
Fuji Photo Film/Sports Illustrated: 36-37
Sports Chrome: 38, 39
Rich Clarkson/Sports Illustrated: 40, 41
Mike King/Sports Illustrated: 45

CRESTWOOD HOUSE
Hwy. 66 South Box 3427
Mankato, MN 56002-3427

TABLE OF CONTENTS

Mary Decker Slaney has been running and winning races since she was eleven years old.

BORN TO RUN

At the age of eleven, Mary Decker Slaney entered her first race.

"We were bored," Mary says, "we didn't know what to do."

Mary was in the sixth grade. She and a friend saw a notice on the school bulletin board asking for volunteers for a cross-country meet.

"I had no idea what 'cross-country' meant, but it sounded like fun," Mary remembers.

When her friend learned that cross-country meant a long race over a hilly course, she dropped out. Mary stayed in. In fact, she led the race from start to finish.

"The race was fun," Mary recalls, "Even if I hadn't won, I would still have enjoyed the competition. But I knew I liked it, and right then it didn't seem like it was going to be all that hard."

"After that, all I wanted to do was run. I just loved the freedom it gave me, " Mary says.

THE CROSS-COUNTRY CHAMPION

Mary was born on August 4, 1958, in Bunnvale, New Jersey. When Mary was ten, she and her family moved to California. It took a while before Mary's parents, John and Jacqueline Decker, decided where they wanted to live. They moved from city to city. Finally, they settled down in Garden Grove, California.

Mary and her mother were very close. At home, Mary's mother decided most things. Mrs. Decker did most of the talking. Mr. Decker was very quiet.

Jacqueline Decker saw something special in her daughter at an early age. She saw that Mary had more than her share of drive and energy. She thought Mary might become a good actress. She even signed Mary up with a talent agency.

Mary, however, had already found her own stage. For her, the track was the only place she wanted to perform. Soon, it became a kind of home away from home.

"I am comfortable on the track," Mary has said. "I have more confidence there than in anything in my life."

By the age of twelve, Mary was entering lots of cross-country meets. She always came in first. She won the Garden Grove city championship. She also won the county and state championships.

THE BLUE ANGELS TRACK CLUB

Though it was difficult, Mary seemed to enjoy training. She ran five to six miles a day, six days a week. After school, she ran for two-and-one half hours before coming home.

She joined the Blue Angels Track Club in Huntington Beach, California. Even with little racing experience, Mary was soon the best runner in the club. She began to

When she first started to run, Mary was a cross-country runner.

run other distances besides cross-country. Her string of first place finishes continued.

One day, Mary set a national record for the thirteen-year-old age group. At the Mt. Sac Relays, she ran 800 meters in 2:17.7. The same year, she ran a mile in 4:55. This was an amazing time for a girl so young.

At five feet tall and ninety pounds, "Little Mary" began out-running all of the other girls her age. Her coach, Don DeNoon, saw that Mary could be a world-class runner. He began entering Mary in open meets. In these races, Mary faced the best female runners in the country. Usually, Mary was the youngest runner in the field.

Mary's whole life began to center on training and racing. She spent hours at Orange High School training with the boys' track team. She often went to Fountain High School to run with the Blue Angels. On weekends, she often competed in several races a day.

Mary feels that she was "born to run."

Though Mary had entered her first race out of boredom, racing had since become much more than a way to pass the time.

"It was a means to early approval," Mary says about running. "It was also therapy during rough times, but it was mainly just such a great physical joy. I knew I was born to run."

Mary's mother was happy that her daughter enjoyed running so much. Before each big race, she always prepared a big plate of spaghetti. This was Mary's favorite dish.

Still, Mrs. Decker worried that Mary might be pushing too hard, too soon. She feared that Mary might soon be "burnt out" on running.

"If my determination and drive stays, I'll keep going, " Mary said at the time. Somehow, Mary knew she wouldn't lose interest in running. "It takes a lot to burn out the human body," she said.

THE GOLDEN GIRL OF TRACK

By the age of fourteen, Mary was being called the "Golden Girl" of track. Few other runners had done so well at such an early age. The best female runner in the country at the time, Francie Larrieu, predicted that Mary would some day rewrite the record books.

As it turned out, "some day" wasn't that far away. Most runners had speed, strength, or endurance. Mary had all three. Her long, easy strides were beautiful to watch. She also had pigtails, braces, and special spunk. Clearly, the best was yet to come.

"You see," Mary said, "I honestly think of running as an art form. Watching a race is like looking at a pretty picture. But it is also something that requires total dedication. I want to give one hundred percent to my sport."

TOO YOUNG FOR THE OLYMPICS

In the 1972-73 racing season, Mary continued to win races. Indoors or outdoors, she won by large margins. Usually, she left the pack far behind. Her main competition, it seemed, was the clock.

Soon, Mary was ranked with the top runners in the world. Mary thought she had a chance to win the half-mile event at the 1972 Olympics. Because of her age, however, Mary was ruled to be too young to compete.

Mary was very unhappy. Still, she continued to make her mark at meets all over America. At the Times Indoor Games in Los Angeles, California, Mary put on a show for her home-town fans. She won one race by over twenty yards. Her time for 880 yards — 2:06.7 — was a new world record.

"I didn't go all out," Mary said later. "I can see going under two minutes, for sure, outdoors."

In the fall of 1973, Mary was invited to join in a world track tour. For several weeks, she ran against top runners all over the globe. She travelled to Western Europe, Africa, and the Soviet Union. While she welcomed the experience, it wasn't always easy being away from home.

"I was only fourteen," Mary recalls.

"Sometimes I felt out of place. It was like having eighty brothers and sisters."

Mary celebrated her fifteenth birthday in Dakar, Senegal.

10

A SPECIAL BIRTHDAY

Mary turned fifteen while the team was in Dakar, Senegal. On her birthday, she and her teammates were in the

hotel dining room. Mary had just finished a plate of spaghetti. Suddenly, a group of black men in robes entered the room.

The men came to Mary's table. Some of them were carrying roses. Mary wondered why.

Then the leader made a hand signal, and the men bowed. Then they gave the roses to Mary. The Premier of Senegal, they said, had learned it was Mary's birthday. They gave Mary a statue. It was a bronze sculpture of an African soldier on a horse.

Mary was so surprised she couldn't speak. She turned red and giggled.

At this point, her teammates joined in. "Happy Birthday," they sang. Mary still didn't know what to say. But her happy tears showed how she felt.

THE PERFECT RUNNER FROM THE HEAD TO THE KNEES

"I really **love** to train and **love** to run," Mary has said. "I don't say I have to run, but hey, I get to run today! So, I don't have to be pushed, I have to be held back."

From the time Mary first began running, the hardest lesson for her to learn has been how **not** to train. In 1970, she once ran seven races in a single week. This included a marathon, which is a race over twenty-six miles long. A while later, Mary landed in the hospital.

Beginning with that seven-race stint at age twelve, Mary learned that injuries would be part of her career. Over the years, she would suffer many of them.

For Mary, physical pain was a price she was willing to pay. To her, the pain of not competing is even greater. As she puts it, "the only time I feel bad is when I can't go out and run."

Still, the limits of Mary's willpower have never matched those of her body. In 1974, she began to suffer a series of crippling injuries. The problems were partly caused by overtraining. Mary believes her changing physical make-up was also a factor.

"I grew from five feet and ninety pounds late in 1973, to five feet six inches and one hundred fifteen pounds by the beginning of 1975." Mary explains. "I didn't know what to do with all this body I had . . . my stride changed. My center of gravity changed. The stresses were different. I was ripe to get hurt."

Hurt — by the tender age of fourteen, it was a word Mary already knew very well. Her training had caused her calf muscles to become overdeveloped. The skin around her calf muscles pinched whenever she ran. Her legs always ached.

The pain got so bad that Mary could barely walk. She searched from one doctor to another for a cure. She tried everything — rest, casts, and no casts. She had X-rays and

Even though she was often in pain, Mary kept training.

operations. She tried powerful drugs that made her legs swell and her hair fall out. Nothing worked.

"At one point," she said, "I was taking twelve aspirins a day. Finally, the pain got so bad I had to grit my teeth. I couldn't walk. Sometimes I felt hopeless and wanted to punch something."

Oddly, the physical gifts that helped Mary run so well were also the cause of her pain.

"People have always described me as the perfect runner from the head to the knees — and glass from there on down," Mary says, pointing to the scars on her shins. "I've got rabbit's feet, with very high arches and narrow heels. They make me an efficient runner, because only my toes and heels strike the surface and very little of my foot hits the ground. But that's also the problem. Because my arch isn't absorbing any of the shock, my heels and shins take all the punishment."

Because of her leg problems, Mary was out of competition for several months. This brought about an even deeper disappointment — missing the 1976 Olympics.

"When you want to do something so bad and you can't, it hurts," she said. "But you can't give up."

MARY FINDS A CURE

Mary graduated from Orange High School in 1976. She then moved to Boulder, Colorado. She got a job selling running shoes in a sporting goods store. Even though she couldn't run, she wanted to stay as close to the sport as she could.

Frank Shorter, the man who owned the store, was a 1972 Olympic champion. "Mary spent most of her time stumping around the store in leg casts," Shorter remembers. "But she was very gregarious and great for business."

At the same time, Mary had accepted a track scholarship at the University of Colorado. As Mary puts it, she ran "just enough" to keep the scholarship.

Meanwhile, she continued to search for a cure. Mary met another runner named Dick Quax. Quax had had the same problem with his legs as Mary. Taking his advice, Mary underwent a special operation. The result was amazing. Within a month Mary was running again! The pain had gone away.

In February of 1978, Mary entered her first major race in three years. At the United States Olympic Invitation Meet in Los Angeles, Mary set a new world record. The distance was 1000 yards. Her time — 2:23.8 — was almost three full seconds off the old mark.

The next year, Mary turned twenty-one. Knowing the 1980 Olympics were only a year away, she quit school. She gave all of her energy to running. She also moved to Eugene, Oregon. This city is known as the track capital of America.

In Eugene, Mary joined a track club called Athletics West. Before Mary, only male runners had been allowed to join.

"They kind of bent the rules for me," Mary said.

Mary was the first female to join Athletics West, an athletics club in Eugene, Oregon.

Coach Dick Brown taught Mary to be more confident.

THE RIGHT COACH

Once Mary joined Athletics West, she began training under a man named Dick Brown. Brown knew that Mary needed a special kind of coach. She needed someone to hold her back — not push her on. She also needed some confidence. Her injuries and Olympic setbacks had discouraged her.

"He was so calming, so confident in me that he was like a father," Mary said about Brown. "And when you've had a family background like mine . . . that's wonderful."

Brown was the first coach to understand Mary's emotional needs. "I could understand how people might have seen her as a spoiled brat, but I knew she wasn't. She's done well with all the attention that's been shown her all her life. But through it all, she's really been searching for a family."

"If we keep you healthy," Brown promised Mary, "no one can beat you."

Brown began to limit Mary's training. He also taught her a new running technique. Because she had alway been a front runner she had never had to develop a finishing "kick." Brown taught her how to build her speed at the finish of a race.

At the start of the 1980 racing season, some people thought Mary was a 'has-been.' She would never come back from her injuries, they argued.

Mary, however, showed that she was far from through. In the period from January 26 to February 22, 1980, she set four new American and World records.

Everywhere she went, crowds flocked to see her run. More than ever, Mary prided herself on looking great when she ran. She always wore makeup and jewelery. Her showmanship was even more polished. She loved to have the crowd on her side and she knew how to win them over.

Meanwhile, her running times got better and better. In race after race, she roared to the front of the pack. And she always had something left to put an extra push into her finish.

"A lot of people don't want the lead," she explained. "But I have confidence in my finish and I like staying out of trouble. The lead is the best way to do it."

THE OLYMPIC BOYCOTT IN 1980

Mary's comeback would have been complete had it not been for something out of her control. In 1980, President Jimmy Carter ordered United States athletes to boycott the Olympic games. This meant that all of the athletes who had trained so hard for four years could not compete.

Mary, along with her teammates, was crushed. For twelve years, she had waited for this moment. Her age, injuries, and now politics, had denied her a chance at "the gold."

In August of 1980, Mary suffered a torn achilles tendon. It would be a full year before she could resume training.

Despite her setbacks, 1980 had been a banner year for Mary. In honor of her achievements, Mary was named the Amateur Sportswoman of the Year by the Women's Sports Foundation of America.

MARY DECKER BECOMES MRS. TABB

"Each time I've been hurt, it's just made me more determined to come back again," Mary has said. "I could be injured tomorrow, and have to take another year off. But I can tell you right now, I'd be back."

In 1981, Mary left the hospital after her third shin operation. She decided to go to a concert. While she was there, someone bumped into her. Falling down, Mary landed on her scars. This forced her to take even longer to recover.

Mary had suffered through one injury after another. Each time, she had been able to rise again to new glory. This time, however, even Mary wondered if she could come back once more.

Mary's road to recovery began shortly after meeting a man named Ron Tabb. Tabb was also a runner. He lived near Mary in Eugene. One night, he decided to knock on Mary's door.

"It was eleven p.m. and I thought he was nuts." Mary remembers. "But I had nothing going on that night, so we went out dancing."

In September of 1981, Mary and Ron got married. From then on, they were together all the time.

Ron knew that Mary needed a special partner. As a full-time athlete, she had lots of needs. She wanted them to travel and train together. She was also a bigger star

In 1982, Mary set a new world record for the mile.

than Ron, so Ron sometimes had to put his career aside for her's.

Ron helped Mary believe in herself again. Along with Dick Brown, Ron told Mary to be patient. He made sure she didn't overtrain. At the same time, he helped her set new goals. Slowly, Mary began to find her way back again.

MARY'S SECOND COMEBACK

Mary set her sights on a comeback in 1982. She began running races again. And, just as before, she won most of the times she ran. Not only that, she was running better than ever before.

By year's end, Mary was the only woman to hold a world ranking in five different events. These events were the 800, 1500, 3000, 5000, and the 10,000 meter events. In Paris, France, Mary entered five events and won them all. Her time for the mile — 4:18.08 — was a new world record.

Less than twenty-four hours later, Mary raced again. This meet was in Eugene, Oregon. She had never run 10,000 meters before. Still, she slashed forty-two seconds off the world record. Amazingly, she had set two world records in less then a day!

Wherever she ran, Mary topped the field. Even her closest rival, the clock, was losing the battle. At one point, she held five American records.

For the second time, Mary was named the top amateur athlete by the Women's Sports Foundation. She was also the first woman ever to win the Jesse Owens Award. This award is given to the top track star in America.

THE DOUBLE-DECKER

By the winter of 1983, Mary had her sights set on a single goal: winning a gold medal at the 1984 Olympics. This time, the games would be held in Los Angeles, California. Mary looked forward to making a winning return before her home-town fans.

Mary and her coach settled upon a game plan for the

year. They wanted her to peak just in time for the Olympics in August of 1984. In the final phases of her plan, Mary would compete in three international events. The first of these was held in Stockholm, Sweden.

When she arrived in Stockholm, Mary hid herself away in a small hotel. She wanted to be somewhere in which "no one could possibly find me." She did this to keep her thoughts on running. As an international star, many people wanted to see her. Interviews and business deals took up lots of her time.

"It was all getting to be too much for me," Mary said. "I needed to get away."

Mary's strategy paid off. When it came time for Mary to compete, she felt calm and relaxed.

The first race was 1500 meters. As the starting gun sounded, Mary got the lead. After the first lap, she was ten meters ahead of the next runner. At the end of the race, she was almost thirty meters ahead. Mary crossed the finish line with a time of 3:57.2. This time was more than two seconds better than the old American record.

On the following Sunday, Mary was in Gateshead, England. Before this meet, Mary announced, "I'm going for another American record."

The distance of Mary's race was 800 meters. Though she wanted to set a record, there was a chance she wouldn't even win. She had caught a cold and her feet were aching. Still, she took her place at the starting line.

A crowd of fourteen thousand fans cheered as the race started. There was stiff wind and Mary was in pain

Mary has often had to run while in pain.

throughout the race. Still, she led the field coming down the backstretch. She knew that a new record was still in reach. Mary gave it all she had as she headed for the finish line.

Mary finished the race twenty-five meters ahead of the pack. Her time was 1:57.60. She had succeeded in breaking the old American record.

Now, it was on to Helsinki.

TRIUMPH IN HELSINKI

The press applauded Mary's Double-Decker" at Stockholm and Gateshead. Meanwhile, Mary moved on to Helsinki, Finland. This was the final phase in her preparation for the summer Olympics.

For the first time ever, outside of the Olympics, all of the world's finest runners were gathering to compete. This meet in Helsinki was called the First World Track and Field Championships.

When Mary arrived in Helsinki, there were some who saw her as an underdog. In Helsinki, Mary would face the world's best runners. It would be her toughest test so far. One Soviet runner, Tatyana Kazankina, had beaten Mary by seven seconds in an earlier contest. Other runners from Russia and Eastern Germany were also highly ranked.

Many people still had some doubts about Mary's finishing power. As a front runner, she hadn't needed to come from behind too often. The European style of running, rough and physical, might wear her down, some said.

Mary was used to running in front of the pack. Experts thought this would cause her trouble in Helsinki.

On top of all this, Mary had recently parted from her husband. Both she and Ron Tabb were competing at Helsinki, however. Some thought Mary's personal problems would ruin her ability to perform.

The first race for Mary was 3000 meters. When the gun went off, Mary took the lead. This time, however, the other runners were right on her heels.

"It was a **good** feeling, compared to being way out in front," Mary said later. "You can't make mistakes, and you sure keep alert. It seemed no time at all before we were coming up to the last lap."

With six hundred meters left, the other runners still trailed Slaney. But with fifty meters to go, Kazankina pulled even. This was a moment many had been waiting for. Everyone wondered if Slaney had enough kick to beat the Soviet to the finish line.

At that point, Mary "took a deep breath, relaxed, and went," out-racing Kazankina to the line by four meters.

"Until that moment," someone said later, "we never knew how good Mary was."

Four days later, Mary was put to another test. This time the distance was 1500 meters. Again, Slaney was up against a tough field. One Soviet runner, Zamira Zaitseva, had been a two-time gold medal winner in the Olympics.

As the race began, Zaitseva tried some rough tactics on Mary. She tried to unsettle Mary. "She hit me practically every stride of the way," Mary said later. "Not obviously, but just brushing elbows, touching shoes."

Mary says that Zamira Zaitseva was often hitting her during the 1500 meter race in Helsinki.

*Mary throws herself across the finish line as Zaitseva
falls to the ground (left), and then runs a victory lap
(right).*

It was an effort for Mary to keep her cool. "I thought
about taking a swing at her, but then I worried about
being disqualified, too," Mary said.

Mary held the lead through 1400 meters. But suddenly,
Zaitseva bolted past her. For two years, no one had ever
seen Mary in second place. With only twenty meters to go,
it seemed certain the Soviet would win.

Somehow, Slaney pulled even again with less than ten
meters in the race. "I caught her because I was so angry."
Mary said.

The finish line was only a few strides away. Tired out,
the Soviet runner threw herself forward. As she tumbled

towards the ground, Mary kept charging on the outside. She pushed her chest forward at the last instant.

"My eyes had been shut," Mary said. "I didn't know I'd won until I saw the replay on the scoreboard."

Mary's triumphs in the 1500 and 3000 at Helsinki capped a very good year. For the first time, she had been almost injury free. She was undefeated in twenty finals. She held all of the American records from 800 to 10,000 meters. She was named Amateur Sportswoman of the Year for the third time. And she was only the sixth woman in history to win the Sullivan Award.

After a busy year, Mary finds time to do some cooking at home.

PREPARING FOR THE OLYMPICS

By the age of twenty-five, Mary had established herself as one of the greatest runners of all time. She had overcome many injuries and personal problems. She had shown an amazing will to win. But in spite of this, Mary still felt a need to prove herself. She wouldn't be satisfied until she earned a gold medal.

"Everyone knows how much I want this," Mary said. "Everyone knows how much I want the opportunity to compete, whether I win or not. It's not something I can show you, except when I'm out on the track."

In July of 1984, just three weeks before the Olympics, Mary's legs were injured again. In the past, surgery was the way to cure it. But time didn't allow this solution.

Mary desperately sought another cure. She took a powerful injection of medicine. The next day, she couldn't walk at all. Still, she put her mind to the task of healing before the competition.

She worked out for a week in a pool strapped in a harness. The harness held her afloat in the water. She ran without touching the botton of the pool. Slowly, her legs healed.

After three weeks, Mary had somehow pulled it off. When the Olympics began, she was ready to run again.

THE 1984 OLYMPICS: THE DREAM BECOMES A NIGHTMARE

On August 10, 1984, 100,000 fans were gathered in the Memorial Colliseum. They were there to celebrate the twenty-third Olympiad of the modern era. For many, this was a day that they had been long awaiting.

On the track below, Mary took her place in Lane One. Beside her were eleven of the world's finest female runners.

Mary had decided to enter only one event — the 3000 meter run. She had made it to the finals. It would be her

Sewing is one of Mary's hobbies.

Mary watches as Zola Budd breaks from the pack.

one and only chance at the gold in over fourteen years of competition.

The starting gun sounded. As expected, Mary surged to the front. Cornelia Burki of Switzerland and Aurora Cupta of Portugal were close behind. Marcia Puica of Romania was there also. Alongside Puica was a seventeen-year-old barefoot runner running for Great

Britain. Her name was Zola Budd.

At the four hundred meter mark, Slaney still had the lead. Her time was two seconds ahead of the world record pace. Slaney kept her lead through the next twelve hundred meters.

Suddenly, Zola Budd began to break from the pack. As a child, Budd had slept with a picture of her idol, Mary

Zola takes the lead (left), and then crosses in front of Mary (right).

Decker, over her head. As she entered the back curve, Budd pulled even with Mary. Coming out of the curve, Budd took the lead.

Soon after taking the lead, Budd crossed over into

Mary's lane. The two runners were separated by less than a stride. They brushed against one another. Mary's spikes drew blood from Budd's left calf. Both runners lost their balance for a moment, but then they recovered.

Mary begins to fall (left), and lies in the infield (right).

Five strides later, Zola and Mary brushed again. This time, Budd's leg swung inside. Mary, in trying to avoid the leg, began to fall. Suddenly she was on the ground.

"The first thought I had was to get up and run," Mary

said later. "But when I made the slightest move, I felt the tear in my hip. It felt like the rest of me was tied to the ground and all I could do was watch them run off."

As Budd continued running, Mary lay on the infield on

her back, tears streaming down her face. "All I felt was the frustration," she said.

Before the race ended, the crowd began to boo. Budd faded and Marcia Pucci went on to win. But for many, the victory was less memorable than Mary's fall.

MARY BLAMES BUDD

"I was running a good race and I hold her responsible," Mary said later at a press conference. "Her foot caught me and I was starting to fall. I should have pushed her, but the headlines would have read 'Decker pushes Budd.'"

At first, the Olympic judges ruled that Budd made an error. She was disqualified. Later, this judgement was changed. The judges believed no one was at fault.

For her part, Budd said, "I am upset that Mary fell, and that the crowd thought it was my fault. I don't know what happened, but she seemed to run into the back of me."

"I really am upset because Mary has always been my idol," she said later.

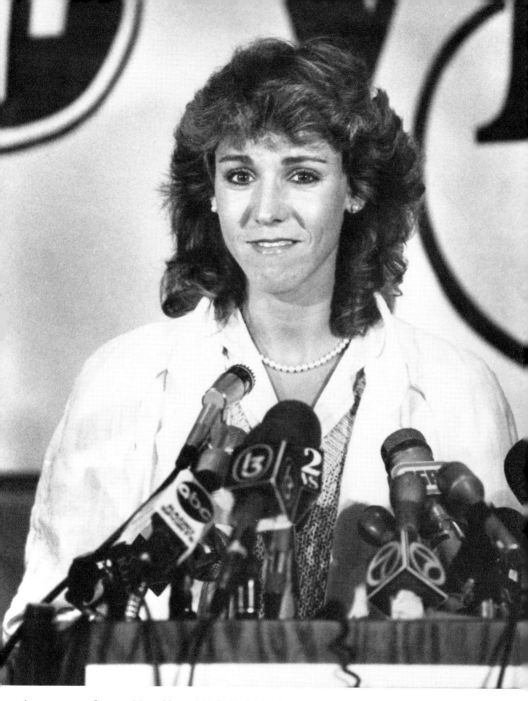

At a press conference Mary blamed Zola Budd for her fall. Later, she said she would never run against Zola again.

THE DREAM CONTINUES: THE 1988 OLYMPICS

After the Olympics, some people criticized Mary. They thought she should not have blamed Zola Budd for what happened. People saw Mary differently then they used to. When she was fifteen and had thrown her relay baton at a Soviet runner who had cut her off, people said she was 'spunky.' When she refused to accept Budd's apology, people said it was "sour grapes."

"As I look back, I've learned a lot about what happened in Los Angeles." Mary said later. "I don't have any hard feelings toward Zola Budd. She was at fault for what happened, technically. But I don't blame her. It was an accident . . ."

"It's bad history; but it's history. I still have the same talents, and I have even more drive now. That's one of the positive things that developed from the incident."

After the Olympics, Mary took about two weeks off. It took several weeks before she recovered from her hip injury. At the same time, Mary was falling in love. Later, she married a man named Richard Slaney. She is now expecting her first child.

At this point, Mary is looking foward to the Olympics in 1988. These games will be held in Seoul, Korea. Mary

*Mary poses for a picture with her new husband,
Richard Slaney.*

*By July 13, 1985, Mary was well enough to win the
1500 meter run in the Paris International Track and
Field Meeting.*

knows that middle distance runners peak later in their careers. Marcia Puica, the woman who won the 3000 meter event in the 1984 Olympics, was thirty-four years old.

"I won't be happy until I win a gold medal," says Slaney, now twenty-eight. "It's something I've always wanted to do. When my running is finished, I want to look back and say I did it. I've put all I had into the sport."

When asked if she would take a guarantee of a gold medal if the price was never being able to run again, Slaney had a quick answer.

"No," she says. "If someone just gives you the medal, what's it worth? To talk about a deal like that just wrecks the sense of the gold. It isn't anything you can buy, it's only something you can win. It's only a symbol of how good **you** are. No, I'd rather take my chances. And," she adds with a smile, "be able to run later on, too."

MARY DECKER SLANEY'S RECORDS

INDOORS

EVENT	TIME	DATE	PLACE	TYPE
800m	1:58.9	Feb. 22, 1980	San Diego	American
880y	1:59.7	Feb. 22, 1980	San Diego	American
1000y	2:23.8	Feb. 3, 1978	Inglewood	World
1500	4:00.8	Feb. 8, 1980	New York City	World
Mile	4:20.5	Feb. 19, 1982	San Diego	World
2000	5:34.52	Jan. 18, 1985	Los Angeles	World
3000	8:47.3	Feb. 5, 1982	Inglewood	World
2 miles	9:31.7	Jan. 21, 1983	Los Angeles	World

OUTDOORS

EVENT	TIME	DATE	PLACE	TYPE
800	1:56.90	Aug. 16, 1985	Bern	American
1000	2:34.8	Jul. 4, 1985	Eugene	American
1500	3:57.12	Jul. 26, 1983	Stockholm	American
Mile	4:16.71	Aug. 21, 1985	Zurich	World
2000	5:32.7	Aug. 8, 1984	Eugene	American
3000	8:25.83	Sep. 7, 1985	Rome	American
5000	15:06.53	June 1, 1985	Eugene	American
10,000	31:35.3	Jul. 16, 1982	Eugene	American

48